Travelling Light

Travelling Light

by

Alwyn Marriage

First published 2025 by The Hedgehog Poetry Press

Published in the UK by
The Hedgehog Poetry Press
5, Coppack House
Churchill Avenue
Clevedon
BS21 6QW

www.hedgehogpress.co.uk

ISBN: 978-1-916830-13-4

Copyright © Alwyn Marriage 2025

The right of Alwyn Marriage to be identified as the author of this work has been asserted in accordance with the Copyright, Designs and Patents Act 1988.

All rights reserved. No part of this publication may be reproduced, stored in or introduced into a retrieval system, or transmitted in any form, or by any means (electronic, mechanical, photocopying, recording or otherwise) without prior written permissions of the publisher. Any person who does any unauthorised act in relation to this publication may be liable for criminal prosecution and civil claims for damages.

9 8 7 6 5 4 3 2 1

A CIP Catalogue record for this book is available from the British Library.

All photography © Alwyn Marriage

for Sophia
who encouraged me to say yes

Contents

AFRICA 13

Internal flight, Africa 15
Why the lame man jumped 16
Korogocho 17
Paying the price 18
The Lord's Army 19
Soroti surprise 20
The joys of making do 22
Any Other Business 23
Present 24
The Offertory 25
And they dance..26
Really cool hotel 27
Counting them...28
White water 30

ASIA	35
Laying the stone	37
Modes of transport in Bangladesh	38
Fingers in	40
Women's literacy class	41
Doubts and consequences	42
Ice cream in Bangladesh	44
Hotel	46
A generous welcome	47
Pop-Nataraya	48
Sewage and saris	49
Addressing a congregation in the tribal area	50
Plantation	51
Kathak dancer	52
Sacred Cow	54
Postcards from Sri Lanka	55
Arriving in Nanjing 南京	56
Hong Kong high rise	57

LATIN AMERICA 59

Schoolgirl, Bolivia 61
Martin 62
Cochabamba 64
Up high in La Paz 67
Two Sundays 68
The exception 69
Giving the horse its head 70
Chain reaction 71

PACIFIC 73

Colourful language 75
Two swims and beauty 76
Kava and tabua 78
Black face of the deep 80

EASTERN EUROPE 83

Pearls 85
The Hermitage 86
Trans-Siberia 87

GENERAL 91

Travelling Light 93
Water map 94
Countries I never visited 96
Business trip 98
Three tragedies 99
Newspaper picture 100
Susila, CSS 101
Sweet charity 102
Sport is an ice-breaker 103
Bed and board 104
Revealing my mantra 106
Flight home 107

FOREWORD

It so happens that very little of my career has been planned, but has rather unfolded with delightful surprises. So it was that, after years of academic work and writing, I was head-hunted to be Chief Executive of two international literacy and literature NGOs. As well as a busy head office and the management of staff and volunteers throughout the British Isles, this involved very extensive travel all over the world – mainly, but not exclusively, to the poorer parts. Everywhere I went, I was met by kindness and generous hospitality and, naturally, learnt a great deal about the politics, education, social networks and religion of the different countries I visited.

The poems in this book revisit that decade spent on the wing, and celebrate some of the wonderful people I met, countries I visited and projects with which I had the privilege to work. I opened bookshops, laid foundation stones, met students, publishers and radio producers, sat on earth floors at literacy classes, preached in cathedrals and tribal chapels, listened and learned, achieved a smattering of different languages, studied budgets and financial reports and developed the strange skill (now lost) of assessing at a glance how many books were in any library I was visiting. To keep costs down, a great deal had to be squeezed into my six-week trips, so sometimes I would have almost daily flights and a different bed each night.

I was welcomed by publishers, indigenous leaders and bishops. I became adept at chasing cockroaches out of bedrooms and received generous hospitality in some of the most challenging slums of the world. I often found the literacy projects the most rewarding part of the work, particularly women's literacy, but also classes for men and women in city slums and rural farms. I was fortunate to get to know some very beautiful places, ranging from the Bolivian altiplano and Chilean glaciers, to palm-fringed Pacific island beaches.

Everywhere I went, I was keen to encourage local writing and publishing, and I developed something of a mission to stop well-meaning people in Britain sending inappropriate books and other goods to countries where they risked doing more harm than good.

The poems are divided into sections according to the continent to which they refer and include a few 'non-work poems' at the end of each section to reassure the reader that I did, occasionally, have days off! The collection concludes with a more general section of poems that are not specific to a particular continent.

AFRICA

INTERNAL FLIGHT, AFRICA

No airport lounge and lengthy wait,
no frisking by security, or luggage
swallowed by conveyor belt.

Instead, we climb aboard
by stepping up onto a wheel
and squeeze into our seats.

A prayer is offered by the pilot
before he taxis down the airstrip
and takes jerkily to the sky.

No need to fly too high,
which means that we can study
the shapes of homesteads,

trace dust roads, count animals
and watch the heads upturned
to gaze at us flying by.

WHY THE LAME MAN JUMPED

Zimbabwe

In that community, disability was shame
so when the longed-for boy was born
with a leg that guaranteed he would be lame

for life, his parents were initially torn
as to whether they should keep the child
or end his short life to avoid the scorn

of friends and neighbours, as their debts piled
up because he couldn't work. They knew
their little boy could not go out to play

with other children, and it soon proved true
that he lived a lonely life, but he spent each day
learning to read and write, and then to teach,

so that in time he became the village school
master and was able with his lessons to reach
the other villagers who in each evening's cool

would gather round him in a rough thatched shed
to practise letters. One evening I joined their class
to admire their new-found skill, while overhead

unknown to all of us a movement on the grass
roof was bringing danger closer to a break
in the thatch. Struggling in the heat to keep

from dozing, the first I saw was when the snake
landed at the lame man's feet, making him leap
into the air then, with a reaction just as quick,
batter the snake to death with his walking stick.

KOROGOCHO

Kenya

A group of sisters
from the local convent
had offered to guide me

seemed more aware
of the dangers we might
encounter than I was

gently suggested that
I should remove my
wedding ring and

wear a head covering
similar to those by which
they were recognised.

After visiting the
informal slum school
and basic library

I was invited to duck
through a doorway into
what at first appeared

to be a dim interior
but which, lit by lamps
and swept clean

felt calm and safe
and where wise women
and happy children

welcomed me warmly with
stimulating conversation
and a generous tea.

PAYING THE PRICE

She used to have an elder sister and a brother,
but now there's no one left to help her
collect the wood and light a fire.

After the man spoke with the village elders
he came to see her sister, test the flesh,
assess her strength and beauty,

and though she wouldn't raise her eyes to see
the visitor, he inspected all her other features
and deemed her worth the price.

There was no choice, no opportunity to exercise
her filial duty, or rebel; the price was paid
and he departed with his goods. The sale

provided money for her brother's fees
at school, until the army came and took
the boy away to train in arts of war.

The money's all been spent, the precious
children gone, leaving only a father's shame,
a mother's grief and a lonely child.

THE LORD'S ARMY

Northern Uganda

An army, obviously,
but impossible to say
what the Lord
had to do with it.

Library and lecture rooms
burned-out and black,
patches of blood still
staining the floor.

An uneasy quiet masks
the trauma of students trying
to recover a vestige of life
in their ruined college.

I stand there, appalled,
recall that even as a child,
I disliked the old hymn
Onward Christian soldiers.

SOROTI SURPRISE

Uganda

Leaving behind the patchwork
of lush jungle, dry sun-baked hills
and villages of round thatched huts,
we circled once above Soroti
then made a steep descent to land.
The engine purred into inactivity
and as the doors were opened
I thanked the pilot and stepped out
into a surreal cinematic scene.

Sun glinting on metal
momentarily confused the eye,
until my sight cleared and a long
line of soldiers appeared, lifting
their gleaming guns into the air
and shouting; while stretched out
in the opposite direction, ranks
of tribal warriors in colourful
traditional dress raised their
weapons in salute.

> What had I done to deserve
> such a reception?

Behind me in the cab, the radio
was spluttering.
A man in uniform hurried
towards me, but his expression
was not one of welcome.
After the most cursory
of greetings he urged me
to accompany him towards
the nearest building,
while the little plane
that brought me here

taxied its way to a far corner
of the airstrip, bearing away
my luggage.

Was this an arrest?
          a surprise party?
                    was I in mortal danger?

Left alone in an echoing hall
I gathered my thoughts, but
could discover no explanation
until through a tiny window
I noticed another plane descend,
larger, smarter and grander than
the one in which I'd arrived;
and when the doors were opened,
there stood the President,
beaming on the serried ranks
of warriors and soldiers.

Later I discovered that
in preparation for the Presidential
visit, strict instructions had been
broadcast far and wide, warning
that no craft was permitted to enter
Soroti airspace; but because of some
irregularity or weakness in radio
transmission, my pilot had not
received the message.

THE JOYS OF MAKING DO

Uganda

In the absence of a building, the shade
of a mango tree will amply accommodate
eighteen to twenty adults in a literacy class

If there is no blackboard, a suitable
bare plank can generally be found
for chalking up the letters

If the young men of the village want
to voice their welcome in music,
they will happily extemporise

with the aid of wooden crates
fitted with flattened bicycle spokes
and tin boxes rattling with stones

If the people then want to offer
a gift, there's a squawking chicken
and her eggs readily available

If I am the recipient of this kindness
it's polite to sit in the back of the car
for the return journey

nursing the chicken on my lap until
I can donate it, with the eggs, to my kind
and generous hostess back in the slums.

ANY OTHER BUSINESS

I prefer not to identify this country

He was smart, urbane, self-confident,
welcomed me warmly and didn't appear
to have any problem with being
interviewed by a woman.
He told me that his daughter had studied
in Britain, had an MSc from an English
university; so when we'd covered all
our business, I asked if I could meet her.
He may have been surprised,
but was too polite to refuse;
so he snapped his fingers, then
sat back as the door opened.
At first I thought that there
was no one there, until
a movement near the ground
drew my eyes down to where
a beautiful woman was crawling
towards us on her knees;
which is why, to the bishop's
consternation, our meeting ended
with me sitting on the floor,
chatting with his daughter.

PRESENT

Tanzania

Sometimes, without forethought,
preparation or experience,
you respond to the present moment
by doing something you've never done before

as when, in a remote village, a man
rushes up to you holding a little one
who is clearly not as fit and able
as he should be, and asks you
to bless the child.

Without hesitating, you comply,
and feel something indefinable
pass from you to the child, while
simultaneously something passes
from the child to you.

You are moved by the trust in
the child's huge brown eyes
and the gratitude sparkling
from his father's face,
and it is all so real, so good,
so natural, that you are left wondering
why we do not perform this simple act
for one another, all the time.

THE OFFERTORY

Kitwe Cathedral
Zambia

A hum approaches from the door at the west end, growing louder until we have to stretch and bend our heads to see what the disturbance might be Then with both pleasure and surprise we see twenty or thirty women coming down the aisle wearing dresses of identical material and style sky blue cotton splashed with coloured traces, and matching head bands framing shining faces. As they process, they begin to sing and sway from side to side in rhythmic, exuberant way. The one in front, bearing high a collection plate, turns, half-way to the altar, so that she can wait for the two behind her, carrying bread and wine and the rest of the singing, swaying, dancing line of Mothers' Union women, singing as they raise their arms in unself-conscious offerings of praise.

AND THEY DANCE

Waiting for hours at the bus stop
for the elusive lift to town,
there's time to talk, to barter,
crack frequent belly-wobbling
jokes, croon a little, ululate
if absolutely necessary
        – and they dance

The warmest welcome awaits
a visitor to the village, where
young men play makeshift
instruments, shy girls peep round
corners and old men nod wisely
while women prepare a feast
        – and they dance

There's a wedding or a birth
to celebrate, or more tragically
a dead child to be mourned;
a local election to be endorsed
or challenged; domestic or
agricultural duties waiting
for attention
        – and they dance

In the cathedral, the offertory
procession takes far longer than
expected, as the women of the
Mothers' Union, in their matching
dresses, sway their way down
the long aisle, scattering smiles
over all the congregation,
        – and they dance

REALLY COOL HOTEL

Zimbabwe

There are various ways
in which hotels display
their wealth and class:

such as deep pile carpets
on the stairs, soft white
fluffy bathroom towels

silver covers on
the steaming dishes,
free coffee and wine

cream cakes for afternoon tea
and an evening menu
of finest international food.

But the Vicky Falls hotel
is the only one I know
where from time to time

a white-gloved waiter emerges
to pour ice into the swimming pool
to cool it down.

COUNTING THEM

Tanzania

Caught unawares, I croaked
with horror as three cockroaches
emerged from underneath my bed.

After a moment's hesitation,
I clutched my shoe and banged
it down three times to squash them flat,

then commented briefly
to my dictaphone
on the interruption.

Half a sentence later
another two emerged
to be similarly, summarily dispatched.

A sixth, poking its snout
into the light, to find what was going on,
found out. *Now I've killed six*, I reported.

From then on, my report
was punctuated by the number
felled upon the battle field.

Some tried to scurry along
the window sill, others squeezed
through the gap under the bathroom door,

and one particularly bold one
winked at me from the metal frame
of my bed, before I flipped

it to the floor and into
kingdom come. *Seven, eight
nine, ten, eleven. Crash Crash.*

Memories of childhood breakfasts:
*Snap Crackle Pop
... Splat ... Splurge.*

*"I visited their office
nineteen, twenty, to meet
the managing director. Twenty one, twenty two."*

This was getting out of hand.
How many could there be in one
small bedroom? I banged on,

each time imprinting
the number on the tape
to be typed five thousand miles away.

That night, before I went to bed,
I reached the number twenty seven,
finished my report and packed it for the post.

Back in Britain, when it reached
my cockroach-free office, I'm told the tape
entertained the staff for half an afternoon.

WHITE WATER

Zambezi

Keep your fingers in,
don't rock the boat,
try not to fall
into the water
or hungry crocodiles
might decide to eat you
for their breakfast.

If we capsize
(which I'm afraid can
often happen) swim
as fast as you can
to the nearest rocks –
checking first that
no crocodiles are
sunbathing there.

I'm afraid it's always
possible to get sucked
down into a whirlpool.
If that happens,
don't panic –
yes, that's what
I said
don't panic.
Let yourself
sink to the very bottom
in the confidence that
then you'll float right
back up to the surface.

Oh, and just before we
climb aboard, can you
confirm that all of you
have signed the
indemnity forms?

I drag my feet.
What am I doing
here? Is it too
late to change
my mind?

Ready?
Here we go.

Suddenly the fear
that dogged my
footsteps as we
approached
the river
is forgotten
in the rush
of foaming
water and
adrenalin.

We're whisked
out into mid-
Zambezi,
spun around
and catapulted
towards the
first steep
rapid
WHOOSH

continued overleaf

(I now see
why they're
called
rapids)

we're in,
over and
through
before
there's time
to shut my
mouth, but
the cry that

escapes
my lips
is not of
terror but
of excitement
and exhilaration

Fear forgotten
I thrill to the
freedom,
the being one
with the surging
water, my body
responding
to the movement
of the boat,
the freedom
and the energy

We see
the other boat
capsize, the
occupants thrash
out towards the rocks,
but then we're past,
we're flying –
as also is
the time
which rushes
far too fast

so that all too soon
it's over and
the realisation
dawns like
the return of
gentle daylight
that we loved
every moment
of the voyage
and survived.

ASIA

LAYING THE STONE

Insert the blade
  disturb the earth
    reveal
a hole, a space,
  an emptiness or lack
that could be filled
  with learning.

Place the stone,
  imagine
a library or reading room
rising, course on course
built on a firm
  foundation.

Wipe hands and smile
at the photographer.

MODES OF TRANSPORT IN BANGLADESH

I was met at the airport by an English friend
for whom going native appeared to mean
driving her *car* as fast as humanly possible
with one hand pressed firmly on the horn
while her other arm circled wildly in the air.
Seat belts? Who said anything about seat belts?

The most common form of transport
is the noisy, wobbly, smelly but charming
tuk-tuk. With at least five hundred of them
chock-a-bloc on the huge roundabout,
it was clear we'd make more progress if
we abandoned it to weave our way on foot.

Perched astride a *motorbike* behind
a volunteer from the Leprosy Mission,
my arms encircled his waist as we covered
many miles in relative comfort, occasionally
attempting snatches of shouted conversation,
while my hands absorbed my new friend's
body warmth through his thin shirt.

If the next stop on the itinerary
is a literacy class in a tiny village,
and the only way to reach it is to cross
the river on a very basic, rope-and-stick
bridge that sways as each *foot* lands,
then obviously that is the route one
has to take; and as long as one doesn't
look down or get sea-sick, the passage
is not only memorable, but also fun.

It's possible to avoid the curfew
by taking the **night ferry**, but
if the *hartel* continues to the next
morning, being met at the quay
will involve having to dodge police
and vigilantes, with the attendant risk
of being stoned or shot.

It goes against English sensibility
to allow oneself to be pulled by
a fellow human being, especially
when the road climbs up a steep
incline. So I probably offended against
every convention by jumping down
to help push the **rickshaw** up the hill.

FINGERS IN

Bangladesh

I never quite understand why I feel such affection for Dhaka. It has everything about it that I've always disliked in terms of noise and chaos and fumes and crowds; but despite all that, it's an undeniably warm, vibrant and fun city. Dashing around in rickshaws and three-wheeler auto taxis is reminiscent of a fairground, though I don't know why more people are not killed every moment of the day. Certainly if a finger were left outside an auto taxi or rickshaw, it would be amputated within seconds!

WOMEN'S LITERACY CLASS

Bangladesh

After travelling deep into the paddy
on a rickshaw, we balanced on a strip
of dry bank between two flooded rice fields,
to cover the final kilometre on foot.

Ten teenaged village girls had been away
to receive three weeks of basic training
in how to read and write and how to teach,
before returning to share their expertise.

We sat on bare ground, chickens pecking among us,
as gradually the corners of saris covering shy faces
dropped away, along with the darkness of ignorance,
revealing new-found confidence and hope.

At the back, beyond the circle of light, the men stood in a ring
looking nonchalant, gazing at their feet,   secretly listening.

DOUBTS AND CONSEQUENCES

If these women learn to read:

they'll become easy prey
to commercial interests, be tempted
by adverts even more enticing
than the glamourous pictures
plastered on city billboards

                                        on the other hand, they'll be able
                                        to set up in business by themselves –
                                        sewing, chicken farming, delivery
                                        vans and administration; earn their
                                        own income, spend it as they wish

they'll fall more under the control
of their Islamic masters, who seek
to limit and constrain them –
might swallow the fundamentalist
treatises of professional clergy

                                        but maybe the realisation will begin
                                        to dawn, that they've been unjustly
                                        fettered by misogyny, that the truth
                                        that's long been hidden from them
                                        is that Allah is for all

they'll read newspapers and
magazines, start to worry
about crime and climate change,
feel that they've been cheated
of knowledge of the outside world

                                        though it's probably better
                                        to know the truth, to learn about
                                        the sins of richer nations that are
                                        hastening the time when human
                                        life will become unsustainable

it's sad to think that soon
they'll be subject to the lure
of western influence, will
realise what they haven't got
and what they'll never be

                      but maybe after the initial shock
                      they'll take pleasure in discovering
                      the wider world, open the shutters
                      to new possibilities, find a voice,
                      express their own opinions.

ICE CREAM IN BANGLADESH

Even before the boat left
I was bombarded by banging
on my door and a stream
of passionate endearments

but as we made our way
downriver, darkness fell and
peace descended, so I climbed
into my bunk and slept

only to be awakened a little
later by a *Scrabble scrabble
scratch* on the pillow beside me.
Alarmed, I switched on my torch

– and screamed, giving the poor
mouse the fright of his life.
He fled, I lay back down
again, embarrassed.

> *I am NOT scared of mice!*

So, having successfully despatched
the visitor, I returned to my slumbers
confident that there was no reason
why I should be disturbed again

– a confidence that proved misplaced
when I was woken for a second time,
caught the mouse in my torch's beam
and screamed.

> *I am NOT scared of mice!*

At least, I reckoned bravely,
I would be calm and prepared
if the visitor returned a third time.
After all, *I am NOT scared of mice.*

But resolve immediately vanished
when my little friend came back
once more to explore the comfort
of my pillow, – and I screamed!

HOTEL

Dhaka

Along the corridor, shadows tremble
at the sounds of scuttling. Occasionally
a door opens to admit or eject a predator
briefly revealing his sheltering prey.
She is someone's daughter or granddaughter,
vulnerable, wide-eyed, full of fear, too shy
to claim a name. In the next room, a ravaged
woman clutches a faded sari to her breast.
She's old before her time, her body wasted,
thin face bruised and thick with paste.
In the relative security of my hired bedroom,
a gecko on his nightly vigil scuttles along
the top of the wall, watches, unphased by
strange ways of humans, gives no warning,
suddenly flicks his tongue out, catches,
with satisfaction, another fly.

A GENEROUS WELCOME

India

So many acts of welcome and respect:
the garland of fresh flowers placed around
my neck as I arrived, embracing me in clouds
of sweetest perfume; the reverent *namaste*;
the kind consideration for a weary traveller;
gifts, unsolicited and totally unexpected;
the sensitivity of local women who brought
a sari to my hotel room and stayed to dress me;
the scarcely-concealed astonishment when I
admitted that I'd never owned a petticoat;
the fine white cotton slip that was immediately
summoned and delivered from the nearest
shop; the final flourish of the *bindi* carefully
imprinted on the centre of my brow.

POP-NATARAYA

Delhi

A shoe-shine boy, who's never
owned a pair of shoes himself,
is picked up from a corner of
the city on mornings when
he dares to leave his post,
relinquish any hopes of pay.

At the Working Children's School,
his sing-song voice describes the relief
of receiving a bowl of rice each day, his
surprised delight in learning and his hopes
for a future in which literacy might, if he's
lucky, lead to work that's properly paid.

With uncomplicated enthusiasm
he offers to dance for me.
A cassette recorder is switched on
and after a brief moment of stillness
his small nine-year-old limbs take up
the rhythm and begin to move.

For ten minutes without a pause
this mini-god responds to ancient
forms of classical dance, refreshed
by modern pop music: footwork,
hand gesture, fluidity of arm
and head all in harmony.

I'm sure he's never been taught
to dance and doesn't expect reward;
but he's clearly pleased to see
the tears of wonder and gratitude
in my eyes as he bows his head
slightly and walks back to his place.

SEWAGE AND SARIS

India

In the absence of toys, children
will naturally play with mud.

Although it's worlds away from
the sweet salt ooze of fresh marsh

there's still silt and sleaze running
in gullies down the centre of the road

launching dreams of ocean voyages
and offering cooling relief for hands,

legs, faces. Best not to wonder
what pathogens and bacteria

thrive in that slime, plaster
those small limbs, get carried

home for tea – if tea there be.
But far more surprising than

childish delight in play-rich
filth is the perfect cleanliness

of the women and girls who
without interfering, clearly keep

a surreptitious eye on the activity
as they pass along this same sordid

track, unaffected by the stench, the
endless challenges of slum life, who

hold their heads up high, walking
gracefully in their spotless saris.

ADDRESSING A CONGREGATION IN THE TRIBAL AREA

India

Public speaking doesn't come
much easier than this.
Men seated before me on my left,
the women on my right, with two
translators positioned at the front
between me and the sea of faces.

The first translator renders
my words into the national
language, then the second
passes it on in the local tongue,
which gives me ample time to plan
my next point and become aware
of what makes these people laugh
or look temporarily confused.

PLANTATION

India

An old planter remembers:
he remembers the train shouting
tea   tea   tea
as the steam driven mini monster
panted up the verdant tea clad slopes,
(the old planter still remembers,
he remembers the sound of tea)

and then he watched it singing
coconut   coconut   coconut
in the first phase of its joyful descent
(joyful, so joyful; so singing and so
joyful)   as it steamed down
to the coconut groves
of the western plains.

Found poem

KATHAK DANCER

India

Kathak attack
tak tak
tak e ta tak

The slow beat intensifies
tak e tak tak
tak tak te ta
the rhythm parts
revealing Shiva
dancing birth and death,
space, time and all eternity
into existence

tap tap,
the sound throws back
an echo; and as he stamps
the ground I catch a sight
of pale soles underneath
his beating feet.

Is this glimpse of gold
the thrill of the hidden
underneath the known,
the kernel deep inside the nut,
the beat that's felt instead of heard,
the mysterious rhythm of the world?

after that act
tak e ta ta te tak
the fact that finally
attracts attention
is that everything that matters
is drawn into the movement
of an answering dance:
the insistent rhythm
reverberating from the trodden earth
stamping the dull, the dark
the devastating
with the hidden truth
of gold.

SACRED COW

India

The river's slow brown water strokes
the cow who stands self-consciously
half-way between the banks,
bending a patient neck to taste
the honey flowing past,
licks her fore-leg, raises gentle eyes
– deeper than the collected swell
of water from the highlands –
to watch the busy action on the banks,
the hurrying passers-by.

The man who stands beside her,
Baptist fashion, lifts the amber liquid,
lets it fall to cool her back and flanks,
the hide delighting in his gift.
She knows that she is holy, set apart
and so accepts solicitude and reverence
as her right.

She bows her head again, the river
endlessly moves onward, seeking
meaning. She stands alone, eternal,
accepting her fore-ordained position,
basking in inward light.

POSTCARDS FROM SRI LANKA

Kandy

scraggy, mildly anxious dogs nose and nibble
their hind-quarters, planted like tripods
or backward-facing troglodytes along the road

where tethered cows, survivors of the long dry heat,
gratefully explore the verdant monsoon verges
with soft, holy mouths;

and over all the Buddha ponders
peace: a lotus poised
in the opening of a smile.

Temple statue

The giant Buddha, poised pale against blue sky,
gleams moon white through the glimmering heat of day,
gathering the people's prayers, absorbing rays of sunlight
to shine with heaven's golden beams at night.

Roadblock

She lay down, rain-expected fashion,
in the road;
ruminated peacefully
while speeding traffic
parted, swallowed her,
rushed on.

Standing on the verge, her calf
looked on reproachfully,
fluttered luxuriant eyelashes
then lowed in a deep, full, strangely adult voice.

ARRIVING IN NANJING　　　南京

China

It's 11.30pm when I clear
Arrivals and finally emerge
into a strangely quiet airport

where there's no welcoming smile, no
placard bearing my name, the logo of my
NGO or project I'm meant to be visiting.

Something has gone wrong! there's clearly
no one here to meet me; I watch the last few
passengers melt into the night and disappear.

For the first time in my life, literacy
fails me. What Chinese characters
might indicate 'Exit', 'Taxi' or even 'bus'?

Blood thumping in my ears reminds me
I'm alone in a totally unknown world, more
foreign here than anyone's comprehension.

Footsteps start to echo emptily, half
the concourse lights are extinguished, far
away a siren laces the silence of the night.

Arrangements made thousands of miles
away start to crumble, are unravelling,
suddenly appear irrelevant.

Outside, rain is splashing the darkness,
and the reflection of red lights on wet
tarmac confuses my mind further

but it's vital that I keep a clear head,
find a novel way to celebrate
my welcome to China.

HONG KONG HIGH RISE

Stainless steel soaring high into grey sky,
appears so slender that if one day the earth
should quake, the towers would simply sway
resisting dangerous friction.

Plate glass mirror walls in blue,
gold, brown and silver catch and then
return their shining still reflections,
repeat each glimmering message endlessly

and though they can't see through each other's glass,
they gaze back at themselves in constant admiration.
Some stop breathing in their corsets,
while others fly free, released in air.

Tomorrow more will rise,
each laced with bamboo scaffolding,
while builders in straw hats work, unconcerned
to find themselves immersed in sky.

Told that when we build such structures
in the country we come from
we encase each building in a frame of steel
to support the workers,

the Chinese shake their heads in disbelief,
aghast. '*We wouldn't trust ourselves
to that*', they say.
'*No give*'.

LATIN AMERICA

SCHOOLGIRL, BOLIVIA

high on the *altiplano*
you follow a donkey track
barefoot, carrying tucked
under your arm, a book
when you are older
you'll wear a bowler hat
drink coca tea, have babies
cook corn in an old clay pot
remember how you used to walk
ten miles to school and back,
and the soft sweet smell left behind
by pack animals trudging the path
ahead of you in bright clear air,
a vulture circling overhead
and a cactus flowering
once in a hundred years

MARTIN
Peru

According to the Foreign Office, travel
to Lima was unsafe, should be avoided;

but I was committed to visiting projects there
and not prepared to alter the arrangements.

OK, if you must, the advice came back,
but don't go out at night, or visit slums.

So - the first evening in the city, I made
my way out to a shanty town by bus,

and climbed the hill through narrow paths
to the women's literacy class at the top

where children ran around, while mothers,
taking up the challenge of an education

after a long day's work, concentrated,
laughed, chatted and uncovered the joys

of reading, writing and juggling numbers
so they would no longer be cheated when

they set up business, secured their independence.
It was all so worth the effort of getting there.

They benefited from the small support we
had been able to give them and were full

of gratitude, but I gained so much more
by meeting such joyful, committed learners.

There was another joy to come. Darkness
had deepened, the class was over,

and as I moved towards the door, a small
boy called Martin took my hand, assuring me

that he was my protector and would guide me
safely to the bus stop. Slowly and carefully

we made our way down through the labyrinth,
a small hand warm in mine, a high-pitched

chatter filling my ears with music. We reached
the road and stood together looking up at stars

until the bus came. He gave me a quick hug
then turned to trace his steps back home.

How old were you, Martin, 10? 11? already
so wise, considerate and strong, although

so small? And I, a vulnerable woman in a strange
place, had never in my life felt so safe before.

COCHABAMBA

High Andes, Bolivia

Two young men
are waiting for me
at the airport,
so I climb into
their car, although
I don't know
who they are.

As darkness falls,
they drop me at a
down-at-heel hotel
deep in the centre
of town, assure me
that they'll return
to collect me at 5am
next morning, then
wave a cheery farewell
and depart.

A crowd of noisy men,
cheering at a television
in reception, parts to
let me through, so that
the woman at the desk can
lead me upstairs to what
must previously have been
a box room, as it's small
and poky and, I am dismayed
to discover, has no window.

To my surprise, despite
incipient claustrophobia,
I climb into bed and sleep
like a lamb – or llama –
until roused by my alarm clock.
I dress hurriedly and go down
to meet the two young men
again.

As we drive off
towards the mountains
they tell me that
our first visit
will be to a nursery.

Baffled, I sit musing
on the back seat,
fairly sure my NGO
has never worked
with Bolivian toddlers.
Nevertheless, I dutifully
use the time to formulate
some sensible questions
in Spanish for when I meet
the nursery staff.

After several hours
in which bad roads
gradually give way to
pot-holed mud tracks
and at one point an open
field, we finally arrive at
the re-forestation nursery
run by a local radio station
we have recently supported.
At this point I decide
not to mention children.

continued overleaf

So instead of inspecting toys
and kindergarten books,
I find myself guided along
lines of eucalyptus, peach
and prickly pear, breathing
clear mountain air and learning
my first few words of Quechua.

UP HIGH IN LA PAZ

Bolivia

It isn't sickness
        and it isn't pain
it's just that, suddenly
each of my limbs is heavy
and the light uncomfortably bright
and although I'm still quite young
        and fit
crossing the room and climbing up
six stairs has become unnervingly
        difficult.

Even locals, apparently,
can suffer from altitude sickness
if they go away for a while
        and then return.
However, I'm assured,
as soon as I've delivered my talk
to the assembled company,
the symptoms can be alleviated
quite quickly by drinking
        a cup of coca tea.

TWO SUNDAYS

Ecuador and Bolivia

International travel brings
so many privileges, including
the opportunity to learn from
adherents of different religions

and even within one's own
birth faith and culture, it's
invigorating to be exposed
to unexpected variations.

In Ecuador, comfortably seated
in a crowded church, rock band
on stage, shiny-suited men inviting
the penitent to the front to be saved –

it wasn't my scene at all; but *hey,*
I can wave my arms in the air,
singing *Brillé Jesús,* as happily
as the next person.

The following Sunday, high
on the Altiplano of Bolivia,
I stayed with a Roman Catholic
priest and nun

and together, in the quiet
solitude of a humble house,
with no questions asked, we
celebrated mass together.

THE EXCEPTION

Mexico
i.m. Pablo Sosa

Many well-intentioned conferences
subject participants to tedious hours
of ill-prepared presentations laced
with cheap red wine and MSG-laden
crisps, interspersed with night time
gossip fed by watching who
might now be flirting with whom.

But I treasure happy memories
of one exception to this rule,
when scores of writers, publishers,
media presenters and journalists
gathered for an international
conference beneath the rumbling
Popocatépetl volcano in Mexico.

Lectures and plenaries are long forgotten
as the main reason for the event's success
lay in daily sessions led by a musicologist
who introduced songs from many cultures,
inspiring us to perform enthusiastically
and unselfconsciously in languages none
of us spoke or had even heard of before

so that, all these years later,
I look back on that one conference
with pleasure and can still
hum snatches of the music
we shared with such gusto then.

GIVING THE HORSE ITS HEAD

Torres del Paine, Chile

I'd ridden as a child, learned tricks
on Janey, the fat skewbald Shetland
pony, who never demurred as we stood
on her back or hung underneath her belly.

You considered horses to be dangerous
and unreliable, had never forgiven Tonka,
from whose back you unceremoniously fell
on a Welsh pony trekking family holiday.

In our party in Patagonia, two men
swore they'd never mount a horse,
even though it meant they'd lose
their chance to reach the summit.

I was relieved and rather proud that you
were the one who eventually relented, who
sat confidently astride your patient mount
as we forded the first river,

then, unlike me, kept your eyes open
as our sure-footed animals gracefully
picked their way across the narrow sliding
scree slope half a mile above the valley

and when we dismounted to complete
the ascent on foot, it was no surprise
that it was you who showed the most
gratitude and affection to your horse.

CHAIN REACTION
Brazil

One moment walking in the gentle dusk,
the next, a heavy body tipping me off balance,
foreign fingers clutching round my throat.

I glimpsed the golden chain that trailed from his hand,
catching and reflecting sparks of borrowed light
like a glittering comet disappearing into space,

and watched as my attacker, also,
faded into darkness, dodging through
the heavy traffic, evading his pursuers.

As the imprint of his fingers faded,
my neck, exposed to evening air,
felt bare, my body jittery.

I checked behind me every other moment
to see who might be following; while he,
lithe and triumphant, left not a glance behind.

Recovering from shock, I felt a surge
of gratitude that he didn't really hurt me
or threaten harm on anyone I love.

He was skilful, swift and agile,
had work to do
and did it rather well.

He didn't take my camera
or the notebook with the only copy
of the poem I wrote today.

And the exchange rate really wasn't all that bad:
I lost a favourite necklace,
he gained a broken chain.

PACIFIC

COLOURFUL LANGUAGE

North Georgia, Solomon Islands

There are worse places to be marooned
than a jetty in the far north of the Solomons,
surrounded by sparkling sea

though, having arrived promptly at nine
and with no boatman yet in sight at ten,
doubts and questions began to trickle in.

At 11, I started to make polite enquiries
and after a number of telephone calls
was directed to the Government office:

*the last bungalow on the left, down
that dusty palm-fringed road.* Here
I met a gentle soft-spoken secretary

who explained with artless charm,
in language that presumably was less
dramatic in pidgin than in English,

that the reason why the boat
had not arrived was that
'the engine's buggered'.

TWO SWIMS AND BEAUTY

Samoa

The memory from a quarter
of a century ago creeps through
the sticky heat of this summer:

I hadn't expected, on a business
trip, to enjoy two perfect swims
in a single day

but after walking, talking, standing
and examining the college perched
high on a hill above the sea,

the Principal's invitation
to take a sea swim down below
was irresistible.

The clear salt water welcomed me,
bathed my hot skin and washed away
all thoughts of work.

It was all so perfect that it seemed
impossible that the experience
could get any better

until I swam deep into the shady
cave and turned to look back out
towards the open sea

where the sun piercing the entrance
sparkled on every grain of salt
bending the light and illuminating

hundreds, or maybe even
thousands, of darting
multi-coloured fish.

Later, visiting a printing press, I was invited
by Dorothy, the young woman who ran the
desktop publishing, to go to the sea with her.

She drove me to a beach where,
in the shade of palm trees,
I changed into a swimming costume

that by western standards was modest,
but which, not surprisingly, revealed
my arms and legs

Dorothy, on the other hand, walked
straight into the sea in her *lava lava*
which streamed out behind her as she swam,

a creature of sea and sun and
golden sand, full of joy, totally
modest and just as totally beautiful.

KAVA AND TABUA

Fiji

I wasn't sure about the gravelly
drink that had to be downed in one.
Was it narcotic, intoxicating, likely
to cause a stomach upset?

But there I was, on the stage,
keen students all watching,
urging me to throw caution
to the soft Fijian winds,

I therefore slowly raised the cup,
took a breath of innocent air before
gulping down what had little taste
but the texture of sea-soaked sand.

If the liquid was alcoholic,
the effect appeared to be delayed,
and so I launched enthusiastically
into an impromptu speech.

Who knows what words dropped from
my lips that day, and whether the applause
that followed was to reward my oratory
or to sympathise with my shame?

Returning to my seat, I smiled with
genuine affection at the audience, fanned
my face, cooled down a little before being
summoned to the front of stage again.

The college principal approached
wreathed in smiles, shook my hand
warmly, made a dignified speech, then
proceeded to a very special presentation.

Thrilled and grateful for the unexpected
honour, I later questioned whether it was
permissible for my gift to leave the country.
I was assured that there would be no problem

and that I should treasure this offering for ever;
since when the sperm whale's tooth, attached
to a length of plaited coconut fibre, has hung,
with happy memories of Fiji, on my study wall.

Fijian tabua: whale's tooth. Wai ni tabua: the string, made of sinnet, a fibre from the coconut tree, representing the coming together of sea and vanua (land) and hence Fijian identity.

BLACK FACE OF THE DEEP

Fiji

Donning goggles to explore
an underwater kingdom
I'd never seen before

I drifted through coloured outcrops
of coral shaped like roses, cauliflowers,
intricate labyrinths

teeming with exotic fish, all flitting past
my mask like birds in ever-denser
shoals that never quite collide.

A benign shark, scattering
small fry like shooting stars,
nodded passing acquaintance

while the shadowy shape
of a ballet-dancing stingray
glided gracefully below me.

Lulled by such warmth and beauty
I was unprepared for the sudden
dramatic meeting when my goggles

brought me face to black face
with a sea snake who was clearly
as startled as I was by our encounter.

In a film there would have been a clash
of music; here all was silent except for
the soft hiss of water in my ears.

We both immediately turned tail, put
as much salt buoyancy between us as
the vast Pacific Ocean would allow.

Later I learned that there's no antidote
to this creature's venom,
but that, fortunately for snorkelers,

these serpents of the deep are not
particularly aggressive, rarely attack
and are easily more shy than dangerous.

EASTERN EUROPE

PEARLS

Estonia

Tallin, pearl of Estonia,
the land where revolution
is achieved by singing

where the hotel used for foreign
visitors is the former headquarters
of the Communist Party

where the higgledy piggledy
mediaeval streets are clean and
the city lapped by Baltic waves

over which I flew when I departed,
looking down on strings of islands,
scattered pearls sparkling in the sea.

THE HERMITAGE

St Petersburg

Arriving the day before my first
appointment in the city allowed
a precious and, I thought, unique

chance to explore a tiny fraction
of the museum which, it's claimed,
would take three months to get around.

Too brief a visit but, by strange
coincidence and alchemy, my pleasure
doubled the next day, when having

finished all our business, my hosts
surprised me with the special treat
of a guided tour of the Hermitage.

TRANS-SIBERIA

Moscow - Novosibirsk - Beijing

When it became necessary
to visit Novosibirsk, I found
there were several reasons why
I didn't want to fly with Aeroflot
and anyway, there was work to do
not only in Siberia but in Beijing too

and I reckoned it would be
both safer and more exciting
to carve a line across the north
of Europe on the Trans-Siberian
railway at a maximum speed
of 30 or 40 miles per hour,

which would also provide
plenty of time to savour
the sibilant,
        somnolent,
                assonant
                        sleepy sound
as the train trundled over the Steppes.

Novosibirsk
Novosibirsk
Novosibirsk
the rails whispered
as we crept out of Moscow
leaving the known world behind

continued overleaf

Novosibirsk
  Novosibirsk
Before long, roads disappeared
as did towns, to be replaced
by mile upon mile of wide
open spaces, interspersed
with burned-out factories.

Novosibirsk
  Novosibirsk
the samovar in the corridor
provided constant tea and coffee,
and when we groaned to a halt
at deserted stations, there was
generally a babushka waiting
to sell us bilberries and cheese.

A plane would probably
have delivered me just as safely
to my Siberian business, but
would certainly not have been
so varied or enjoyable.

Three days to Novisibirsk,
    three days of meetings,
        then four days on
            towards the rising sun.

A woman without a visa squeezed herself
into a cabin bursting with wellington boots
to sell in China; but at Mongolian passport
control, officials escorted her, wailing,
from the train to meet *'the Commandant'*,
leaving the boots to travel on alone.

Gradually, a sense of camaraderie
emerged among the passengers,
especially when the train's supply of
food ran short, leaving only smoked
salmon and Russian champagne,
to be served for every meal.

Outside, the scenery changed
from steppe to taiga to the vast
expanse of Lake Baikal, before
opening out into the Gobi Desert,
where a former preconception
floated off into thin air

as I discovered that instead of yellow
sand or brown earth, the desert was
a softly blushing green, providing
an idyllic backdrop to yurts, herds
of camels and bareback riders
galloping wildly off into the distance.

At the border between Mongolia
and China, the whole train, with
all its passengers, was lifted up
for several hours of the night
as the bogies were changed
to narrow gauge.

Glimpses of the Great Wall welcomed
us, inviting the train to weave nearer
then further off then near again. A little
later, domesticity crept towards us as tidy
gardens started to snuggle up towards
the tracks, suggesting Willow Pattern

continued overleaf

and all too soon, the gentle rattle
of *Novosibirsk* and the comforting
soft sway of seven days' train
journey were jolted from us
as we came up against the buffers,
blare and noise of Beijing Station.

GENERAL

TRAVELLING LIGHT

As airline passengers, we often face
having to lift our luggage into a high rack,
so try to travel with the lightest case
possible, by being careful what we pack.
Enough clean underclothes to last three days
will generally suffice if washed each night,
plus a blouse that, worn in different ways
looks leisurely by day, formal at night.
Even when we journey to the ends
of human habitation, we soon find
opportunities to make new friends
and learn to trust that most people are kind.
Discovering this not only brings delight,
but gives new meaning to our *travelling light*.

WATER MAP

In Tanzania
even though my host was
Chief Executive of a major
company, we had to cross
two fields, with buckets,
to collect our water.

In India
anything we wished to eat
had to be washed and rinsed
in water that had been
thoroughly boiled.

On the Eastern European train
crossing Siberia, drinking water
came in plastic, but tea was
constantly available on-tap
at the samovar in the corridor.

One of the treats of a Patagonian
boat trip, long before we realised
that glaciers were retreating,
was carving off a tiny lump
of ice to cool our drink.

In the slums
where water flowed down
gullies in the road,
we had to hope it wasn't
destined for drinking.

Anyone who has spent time
in areas of drought will find,
on returning to Britain, that
they are painfully aware of the
profligate wastage of water,

for even though water
covers 71% of earth's surface
and gushes in unstoppable
energy at Victoria, Niagara
and Iguazu, puts a damper
on English summer picnics
and thrashes and crashes
constantly against our shores,
it is precious and in its fragility
as well as it sheer exuberance,
is not a bad metaphor for life.

And in our hearts we know
that when we have dried up
all our rivers, polluted seas
with sewerage and plastic
and turned our rich green land
into dry desert, we will be
faced with the discovery
that without earth's precious
liquid resource, humanity
is doomed.

COUNTRIES I NEVER VISITED

During the nineteen nineties
I travelled far and wide on work
several times a year,

so people sometimes formed
the impression that I'd visited
every country in the world,

which certainly wasn't true.
For a start I only went
to the poorest places,

so anywhere rich, posh
or cockroach-free remained
outside my experience.

I always wanted to go to Japan,
see blossomed shrines and reverently
imbibe ritual tea.

Papua New Guinea intrigued me
because not so very long ago
they used to eat people there.

I hoped in vain to visit the remote
island of Kiribari, with the strange
pronunciation of its name

and there was a reason why, despite
its reputation for crime and corruption
Nigeria was on my bucket list.

At school, one of my friends
was a Nigerian princess, whose
father had many wives,

and who therefore enjoyed
the company of more siblings
than she could count.

This led me to imagine
that the whole of Nigeria
was full of beautiful royalty,

but I never got the chance
to test that theory, and was sad
years later when I heard
that she had anglicised
her romantic African name
to the more prosaic Victoria

... and although my travels took me
to so many African countries,
I never got the chance to visit Nigeria.

BUSINESS TRIP

In those days, twenty or thirty
years ago, I would generally
be away from home for six weeks
at a time, with no access to any
news or communication,

so I never heard
  who had died,
  swapped partners,
  moved house,
  lost or gained
  their fortune,
  or even what Party
  was in Government.

When I returned
ignorant of all that might
have happened since I left,
I was thrown back into life,
and sometimes only discovered
months later, often by committing
a *faux pas*, what I'd missed.

If I were to undertake
such travel now,
my husband could,
if he so wished,
let me know
what he ate
for lunch.

THREE TRAGEDIES

Fortunately, most of us
do not encounter murders
in the course of normal life;
and I'm glad to say that
when I have, my safety
has not been compromised.

In Johannesburg
I was the guest
of a community of monks
none of whom ever raised
a hair (which, to be honest,
most of them hadn't got),
when night after night
the streets outside their house
became a grave for the unwary

In Caracas
where, unusually,
I stayed in a gated hotel,
a man was murdered
a few streets away
from the room where
I slept in safety. He was
killed in cold blood
for the questionable prize
of second hand pair of shoes.

In Quito,
which always seemed
to me so peaceful and
secure, a lovely woman
I had met on business
was killed the night I left
and I only heard
the tragic news as I was
travelling to Galapagos.

NEWSPAPER PICTURE

Please don't show me another picture
of an anguished mother weeping for her child.

I already know what grief feels like, and how
most of us look when overwhelmed by tears,

so I'd rather you didn't publicise her raw emotion
which you can't feel and isn't yours to share.

You really haven't any right to splash
this image over the newspaper's front page.

You can share the story by all means, but keep
the prying eyes of photojournalists at bay.

Just let this unhappy woman retain her dignity,
and live to recover from the pain she feels today.

SUSILA, CSS

Our visitor had filled the washing line with saris, great
white billowing sails that sheltered the lawn from the sun.

When offered a cup of tea or coffee, she found it impossible
to make up her mind, explaining that such choices

were contrary to the vocation in which she'd long ago
committed herself to a life of mute obedience.

So now, the forty years in which she'd never had to make
decisions had rendered her incapable of choosing.

But when I visited her a few years later, I myself
witnessed that when a poisonous snake emerged

from the paddy at her Bangladesh compound,
her decision to kill it was swift and sure.

SWEET CHARITY

she sits there listening to tales of drought in Rajastan
watches the screen, entranced, as files of saris
weave multicoloured threads across the desert,
each elegant lady balancing a pitcher on her head

her crumbly heart is caught up in concern
for the plight of such beautiful people far away
and as so many times throughout her life
she counts her blessings, wondering

how she would cope in her declining years
if like them she had no water:
how would she wash her stockings out at night,
or make the tea?

she digs into her musty handbag, finds the envelope
with this week's pension in it, intends to share
her meagre means with those who are even poorer
by making a donation to the cause

but caught off balance by the speed at which
the collection comes towards her,
she tears the packet open in a fluster
and empties all her money onto the plate.

Don't mention to her the wealth of modern India,
or suggest that providing water for these citizens
would be a worthier way to spend rupees
than competing with other countries in the arms race.

SPORT IS AN ICE-BREAKER

They meant it kindly,
saw it as a way of making
conversation with a traveller
from Britain.

Do you like sport? they asked,
*Yes, very much: tennis, swimming,
rowing, long distance walking –
you name it.* They looked baffled:

*But what team do you support?
Do you watch football, rugby, cricket on
the television? Which side do you cheer?*
Now it was my turn to be confused;

I haven't got a television, don't know the names
of footballers, have no idea of winning teams,
or leagues or relegation. And anyway, I haven't time
to watch, because I'm out enjoying sport.

BED AND BOARD

Meals are for conversation,
companionship and culinary
adventures; while bedtime
comes as sweet relief to ease
tired limbs and minds

but there are occasions
when neither brings relief
as unfamiliar tastes and
varying standards of hygiene
pose a challenge for the traveller:

                            such as
                  when lumps of congealed
                  chicken blood are served
                  to life-long vegetarians
                      at a celebration
                          feast

                          or when,
                    preparing for bed,
                      one stands,
                  helplessly witnessing
                the remorseless march
            of a line of large black ants
            streaming up the bed post.

If, as darkness falls,
exhaustion has not overcome
the unremitting heat, or helped
to hide the torn mosquito net,
the cockroach highway through
the bathroom door,

then a yearning
for the bed and board
of home kicks in
and however fascinating,
exciting or rewarding
the visits one is privileged
to make to far-flung places,
an unwelcome hint of
home-sickness creeps in.

REVEALING MY MANTRA

Golden Shovel *

Some occupations are not suitable for cowards
and even brave people generally don't wish to die.
For instance, though international travel has many
delights and can be problem-free, there are times
when travellers pause to take deep breaths before
embarking on adventures they know could risk their
personal safety or, *in extremis,* lead to their deaths.
At such times I, personally, found courage in the
recitation of a mantra first spoken by the valiant
Caesar in Shakespeare's play. In danger he never
lacked the wine of courage, so I hoped to taste
the same spirit, accept with dignity the wisdom of
words that wouldn't change my attitude to death
(which most of us consider best avoided), but
might help me face an end that happens only once.

* *In a Golden Shovel, a quotation is revealed by reading down the last word of each line*

FLIGHT HOME

brown noise strikes
a threatening tone
then lulls towards sleep

dark blue flight blankets
match reclining seats, offering
a tantalizing mirage of comfort

outside the window a paler blue
fingers the soft tops of clouds, plucking
wisps from a fluffy white pillow below

we are pulled along a smooth line stretching
from as far back as we can remember,
towards the far-off dream of home.

ACKNOWLEDGEMENTS

Black face of the deep	Not a drop: Just Oceans of Poetry, Beautiful Dragons 2016
Chain reaction	Wildfire Words, October 2022
Kandy	*Touching earth*, Oversteps Books, 2007
Kathak dancer	The Journal, Spring 2018
Newspaper picture	International Times, 2020
	Possibly a Pomegranate, Palewell Press, 2022
Paying the price	Art saves lives International, 2016, with an interview with me
	I am not a silent poet, July 2015
	Possibly a Pomegranate, Palewell Press, 2022
Pearls	Poetry Wivenhoe, March 2025
Plantation	Poetry Wivenhoe, November 2024
Pop-Nataraya	Dreich, November 2024
Sacred Cow	Wildfire Words, March 2023
Schoolgirl, Bolivia	*Dedalus,* 2016
	Possibly a Pomegranate, Palewell Press, 2022
The joys of making do	Dreich, November 2024
The Lord's Army	Poetry Wivenhoe, January 2025
Women's literacy class	Selkie: States of Transformation, 2019

With thanks to Charles Elliott who, in the face of my reticence, persisted three times in his efforts to persuade me to accept the appointment of CEO.
Thanks to Hedgehog Press for awarding me the prize in their Full Collection Competition
and
Thanks, as ever, to Hugh for his constant love and support. He never complained about my regular six-week trips abroad, and because he was prepared to take occasional unpaid leave, we had some very exciting rendezvous in far-flung places.

BY THE SAME AUTHOR

Poetry

Possibly a Pomegranate: Celebrating Womankind (Palewell Press)
Pandora's Pandemic (SPM Publications)
In the image: portraits of Mediaeval Women (Indigo Dreams)
Notes from a Camper van (Bellhouse Books)
festo: Celebrating winter and Christmas (Oversteps Books)
Touching earth (Oversteps Books)
New Christian Poetry, ed (Collins Flame)
Beautiful Man (Outposts)

Fiction

The Elder Race (Bellhouse Books)
Rapeseed (Stairwell Books)

Non-fiction

The People of God (Darton Longman & Todd)
Life-Giving Spirit (SPCK)
Bible Best, ed (FTM)

e-books

Chiara (Cut)
William Harvey's Visitor (Cut)
The Elder Race (Kindle)

BIOGRAPHICAL NOTE

Alwyn Marriage has been a university philosophy lecturer, magazine editor, an environmental consultant, and chief executive of two international literature and literacy NGOs. She is managing editor of Oversteps Books and a research fellow in the Department of English at the University of Surrey.

Her previous books include poetry, fiction and non-fiction. She is very widely published in magazines, anthologies and on-line, has won several prizes for her work and gives readings and lectures all over Britain and abroad.

www.marriages.me.uk/alwyn

www.ingramcontent.com/pod-product-compliance
Lightning Source LLC
Chambersburg PA
CBHW061228070526
44584CB00029B/4029